AMERICAN FOOTBALL

Withdrawn

HOW TO PLAY

AMERICAN FOOTBALL

BARRY CAWLEY
CHARLES BROGDEN

Published by Guinness Books
33 London Road
Enfield
Middlesex EN2 6DJ

Produced and Designed by Mander Gooch Callow

Illustration: Sharon F. Gower

Printed and bound in Great Britain by
Hazell Watson & Viney Ltd., Aylesbury

British Library Cataloguing Publication Data

      Cawley, Barry
        How to play American Football.
        1. American Football
        1. Title 11. Brogden, Charles
        111. Series
        796.322

ISBN 0-85112-376-7

Contents

Introduction

The Aim of the Game

The aim of American Football is the same as any other game, that is to beat your opponents. In the case of American Football this is achieved by scoring more points than your opponents, these are obtained by four methods (under NFL rules):

> Touchdown for 6 points.
> Point After Touchdown (PAT) for 1 point.
> Field Goal for 3 points.
> Safety for 2 points.

THE REFEREE'S DECISION

Touchdown,
extra point or
field goal

Safety score

Points are usually scored by the Offense but the Defense can get on the scoreboard with a Touchdown (following a turnover of possession) and a Safety (when an opponent has been caught in possession in his own end zone).

American Football is very much a game of strategy and although every play is carefully planned and choreographed, to ensure that every team member does his job, there is still that prospect of the unexpected – that special talent a player has to 'break the game open' by doing something instinctively and so fooling the opposition and sometimes his own team mates!

The strategic planning of American Football is sometimes compared to a war game, with the ball as a marker of the team's position. Aerial and ground attacks are compared to the passing and running plays and territory is gained and lost accordingly. A battle is won when a Touchdown is gained, but the war continues until the final whistle. Throughout all of this 'organized mayhem', is appreciation of the opponents' talents and without exception, sportsmanship prevails in the world's toughest sport.

The Role of the American Football Team

Teams within a Team

An American Football team is divided into three smaller teams: an Offensive team, a Defensive team and a Kicking or Special team. Each team or unit has specific responsibilities, and therefore the players within those units are trained to fulfil their tasks and rarely interchange between Offense and Defense. However there are those special players who have the ability to do this.

The Roster

The combined Offense, Defense and Special teams or units constitute the playing roster of 45 game eligible players (under NFL rules). However additional players are under contract to the team, and available if necessary, under the heading 'Injured Reserve'. These are players who are injured or who have been retained by the team, but are not on the eligible playing roster.

The numbers

The numbers that players wear do have a direct relationship to the position that each plays on the field. The only exception to this is if a player was allocated a number in the NFL prior to 1972. He would be able to retain his original playing number which may not relate to his playing position today.

The normal numbering would be as follows.

1-19 Quarterbacks and Kickers
20-49 Running Backs and Defensive Backs
50-59 Centers and Linebackers
60-79 Defensive Linemen and
        Interior Offensive Linemen.
80-89 Wide Receivers and Tight Ends
90-99 Defensive Linemen

LAW-BREAKER
All players shall have individual numbers from 1-99, a) on a scrimmage down at least 5 Offensive players on the line of scrimmage shall be numbered from 50-79, an exception to this is during a scrimmage kick formation. b) no 2 players of the same team shall participate in the same down wearing identical numbers. c) the numbering of an individual player shall not be changed during the game in an attempt to deceive opponents, unless that player has informed the referee.

THE REFEREE'S DECISION
Failure to wear required equipment.
Time-out charged to offending team

The Offense

Offensive Unit Objectives

The Offensive team's objective is to score points, whether by Touchdown or Field Goal, once they have gained sufficient yardage towards the opposition's end zone. Field position and ball possession are vital to the Offensive team. The Offense has to have seven men on the line of scrimmage. The objective of point-scoring is rarely achieved in a single play, the Offense has to have the ability to move the ball down field in a series of running and passing plays. The Offensive team keeps control of the football by obtaining or making 'first downs'.

From receiving the ball, the Offensive team has four 'downs' or attempts to make 10 yards. This requirement is measured by two chain markers and a down marker located just off the playing surface on the side-lines. When the Offense takes control of the ball, one chain marker is placed in line with the ball and the other is stretched towards the opponents' end zone. The chain between these two markers is ten yards long. The Offensive team must retain possession of the football and gain the ten yards required, in one, two, three or four attempts, and so maintain their drive towards their opponent's end zone. If the Offense fails to make the 10 yards required on their first attempt, the down marker will be placed laterally to the position of the football, marking the distance required to obtain that 10 yards. In other words if 2 yards is gained on the first attempt, the down marker will be at 2, and two yards in from the first chain marker, giving us the position of 2nd down and 8. In other words, the Offensive has its second attempt with 8 yards required to gain 'first down' once again. This ritual continues as long as the Offense continues to gain first down. Should they fail, possession will be relinquished to the opposition.

A description of an imaginary drive can be found at the end of this section.

THE REFEREE'S DECISION
First down.

The Roles of the Offensive Players

Center/Tackles/Guards
These three positions are described as the core of the Offensive line.

The Center's first task and responsibilty is to successfully 'snap' the ball between his legs to the Quarterback, who is generally standing directly behind him. Only when the snap is successfully completed

LAW-BREAKER
The ball shall be put in play by a legal snap unless the rules provide for a legal free kick.

THE REFEREE'S DECISION
Illegal formation, false start Penalty — 5 yards

can the Center concentrate on his secondary role to
block his designated Defensive Lineman or Linebacker.

On either side of the Center is an Offensive Guard
and an Offensive Tackle. Their role for the Offense is
to block their opponents and so prevent them from
tackling either the Quarterback or the ball carrier. Size
and strength are essential characteristics of an
Offensive Lineman. They never run the football or
indeed touch it, except when the ball has been
'fumbled' or during some sort of trick play.

Split End/Tight End

The Split End and Tight End are the players on each

end of the Offensive line. Although he frequently
changes sides, the Tight End will align from a 1 -3 ft
gap outside one Offensive Tackle, and the Split End
from 7-15 yards from the opposite Offensive Tackle.
The Tight End is always stronger and bigger than the
Split End. His job varies as he is used as a blocker
when the Offense is running the ball, and as a receiver
when the Offense is passing.

The Split End, on the other hand, is leaner and faster
and as he is used primarily as a receiver when the
Offense is passing, he must be able to catch.
Height is an advantage in a Split End.

The Quarterback

The Quarterback is considered to be the general of the
Offensive team. He will call the plays in the huddle
and he will call the count. He receives the ball from the
Center on the snap and he executes the play, whether
it be run or pass. He is usually the captain of the
Offensive team. His characteristics are intelligence,
durability, a strong throwing arm and agile feet with
speed and finesse. Most coaches will also feel that the
Quarterback should be tall, at least 6 ft.

The Flankerback

The Flanker can be aligned in a variety of positions on
the football field, either on the side of the Split End or
outside the Tight End. The only requirement is that the
Flanker be positioned behind the line of scrimmage.
His primary role is pass reception, although he may be
used on a sweep or on a trap. The Flanker's
characteristics are similar to those of the Split End,
tall, fast, agile and with the added ability to catch
the football.

The Running Backs

Running Back is a general term given to two positions.
Fullback and Halfback or Tailback.

The Fullback

The Fullback should be thought of as the bulldozer of the Offensive team. His responsibilities include lead blocking for the Halfback or Tailback, as well as making powerful, short yardage runs, in an attempt to gain his team a first yardage down.

The Fullback's characteristics should be size and strength as well as agility and speed. He needs the strength of an Offensive Lineman and the speed of a Tailback.

The Tailback or Halfback

He is the primary rusher of the Offensive team. His responsibilities are to run the ball anywhere that the play has been designated. This may mean powering through the middle of the Linemen, or sweeping around the Ends in an attempt to gain as much yardage as possible, as well as acting as a secondary or safety valve receiver.

His characteristics should be agility and speed, he must be as fast as a Flankerback or Split End, with the durability or strength of a Fullback. He should be able to catch the ball and throw it almost as well as the Quarterback, when the team attempts trick plays. All-in-all the Tailback or Halfback is probably the closest to the team's all-rounder.

Offensive Techniques

The term technique when applied to American Football includes not only the manner in which the player holds or passes the ball, but also the stance or position he adopts at the start or kickoff and the manner in which, if that is his role, he blocks or tackles his opponent. It also covers the position he takes on the field, with whom and against whom he is aligned.

Center/Tackles/Guards

As described in the role of these players, their primary responsibility is to block. The technique each uses will vary depending on the type of block required. In addition the stance of these Offensive linemen is all important and can vary depending on the play called in the huddle.

Effective and efficient blocking can be the most important and skilful job on the field. If it is done incorrectly, then the play will surely fail.

There is a lot more to blocking than sheer strength,

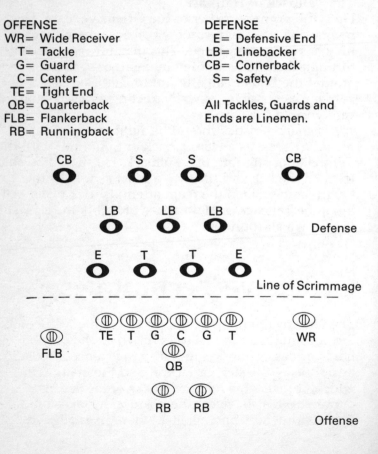

OFFENSE
WR= Wide Receiver
 T= Tackle
 G= Guard
 C= Center
TE= Tight End
QB= Quarterback
FLB= Flankerback
RB= Runningback

DEFENSE
 E= Defensive End
LB= Linebacker
CB= Cornerback
 S= Safety

All Tackles, Guards and Ends are Linemen.

CB   S   S   CB

LB   LB   LB

Defense

E   T   T   E

Line of Scrimmage

TE T G C G T   WR
FLB   QB

RB   RB

Offense

although of course this does help a great deal. Timing, positioning and agility are just as important as strength, if a defender is to be kept at bay. The Offensive Lineman has two definite categories of blocking assigned to him, Run blocking and Pass blocking. On a Run block, his aim is to clear a path for the ball carrier. On a Pass block his intention is to

---

LAW-BREAKER

No player may hand the ball forward except during a scrimmage down under certain circumstances such as a) an Offensive player who is behind the line of scrimmage may hand the ball forward to a back field team mate who is also behind that line of scrimmage. b) an Offensive player who is behind the line of scrimmage may hand the ball forward to a team mate who was on the line of scrimmage when the line was snapped, provided that the team mate left that line position by a movement taking both feet, that faced him towards his own endline and was at least 1 yard behind the line of scrimmage on receiving the ball.
A forward pass is illegal when a) the Offensive team's passing player has passed the line of scrimmage. b) if the ball has been turned over during a scrimmage down, for example if a Defensive team has intercepted the ball and then attempts a forward pass. c) if the offending team attempts a second forward pass during the same down. d) if the Offensive team intentionally throws the ball into an area not occupied by an eligible receiver, in an attempt to save loss of yardage or to conserve time.

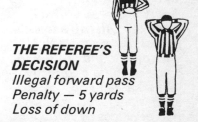

THE REFEREE'S DECISION
Illegal forward pass
Penalty — 5 yards
Loss of down

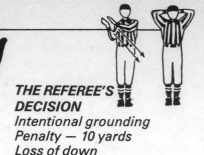

LAW-BREAKER
A backward pass is illegal when a) a runner intentionally throws the ball backwards out of bounds to conserve time. b) when the snap is passed directly to a Lineman.

THE REFEREE'S DECISION
Intentional grounding Penalty — 10 yards Loss of down

protect the Quarterback at all costs, preventing the Defensive players from penetrating their Offensive line. The key to this is good team work and good positioning. On running plays, the Offensive Linemen will have several blocks to choose from.

The stance
The stance is established before the snap. Usually using a three point stance, an Offensive Lineman can power forward, using his legs for impetus and so drive up with his arms into his opponent.

The drive or shoulder block
The basic and most common block in Offensive football is the drive or shoulder block. The most important elements of this block are the approach, the delivery of contact and the follow-through.

LAW-BREAKER
A forward pass is illegal when the Offensive team's passer throws the ball directly into the ground to conserve time or directly into an area unoccupied by an eligible receiver to save potential loss of yardage.

THE REFEREE'S DECISION
Intentional grounding Penalty — 10 yards Loss of down

The Offensive blocker must explode at the snap with speed and control. On the approach, the player must drive off his rear foot and aim his head directly at the chin of his opponent. He must make contact with his head, bringing his forearm and head upwards, in a driving motion into his opponent. At the same time, he must maintain movement by following through, with short powerful steps and so drive his man away from the ball carrier. To enable the Offensive man to maintain his balance, he must try to keep his feet about the same width apart as they were in his original stance. As the Defensive player moves away, the blocker takes that man in the direction of his angle of delivery. By focusing his head on his opponent and driving with his head, the drive blocker can make sure that he makes contact with the Defensive man whichever direction he takes. As the Offensive man drives out at his opponent's chin, the Defensive man will naturally have risen and the blocker will drive into his opponent's chest and shoulder.

The Offensive Lineman must also attempt to drive into his opponent as fast as he possibly can, for the sooner he drives into his opponent, the easier it will be to control his man.

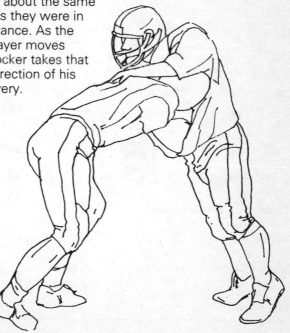

The butt block

By firing out at the Defensive Lineman in an upwards, driving motion, the Offensive blocker should hit his opponent at an angle just below his neck. The Offensive blocker's aim should be to butt the man hard and keep pushing him away.

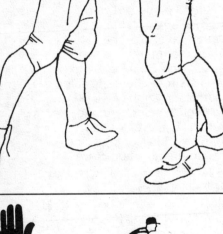

LAW-BREAKER
The player of the receiving team who has made a valid, invalid or illegal signal for a fair catch and does not touch the ball shall not block or foul an opponent during that down.

THE REFEREE'S DECISION
Illegal blocking below the waist
Penalty — 15 yards

LAW-BREAKER
Offensive players positioned more than 7 yards in any direction from the centre of the Offensive formation are prohibited from blocking below the waist until after the ball has been advanced beyond the neutral zone.

THE REFEREE'S DECISION
Illegal blocking below the waist
Penalty — 15 yards

The cut-off block
This is used to prevent pursuit.

The blocker should make his first step in the direction of the man he is assigned to block. He should push out with his rear foot and throw his arms, shoulders and head beyond the far leg of his opponent.

He should always ensure that his arms, shoulder and head are in front of the Defensive pursuer.

The open field block

If the Offensive Lineman's aim is to floor his opponent and not just keep him at bay, then this form of blocking is commonly used.

In this instance, the Offensive Lineman will simply aim at his opponent's belt buckle, pulling his head into his neck before contact to avoid personal injury. Once contact has been made, he should maintain momentum and angle his body through his opponent.

LAW-BREAKER
When a ball is loose no player, offense or defense, can grasp, pull or tackle an opponent.

THE REFEREE'S DECISION
Holding
5 yard gain
Automatic first down

LAW-BREAKER

A team mate of a ball carrier or passer may legally block with his shoulders, hands, outer surface of his arms or any part of his body. He must not hold or illegally obstruct as follows: the hand and arms must not be used to hold, pull, or encircle in any way that illegally prevents an opponent from tackling the ball carrier or passer. The hands or arms must not be used to hook, lock or clam an opponent. a) the hands and arms must not be used to deliver a blow, nor should the hands be locked together during a block. b) a cross body block or open field block is legal if there is no contact with the hands or arms around the opponent.

THE REFEREE'S DECISION
Illegal use of hands, arms or body
Penalty — 10 yards

LAW-BREAKER

No player shall kick a loose ball, a forward pass or a ball being held for a place kick by an opponent.

THE REFEREE'S DECISION
Ball illegally touched, kicked or batted
Loss of down
Unsportsmanlike conduct
Penalty — 15 yards

The pinch block or double team block

This type of block, using two men to drive one Defensive man back off the line of scrimmage, is normally used in power or short yardage plays.

In this double team block, the Guard will take responsibility for eliminating the Defensive player's charge and preventing his penetration. The Tackle on the other hand, will step in faster and prevent the opponent from squeezing between the Guard and himself. His second aim is to prevent the Defensive man from rolling out of the block.

This block is done most effectively when the Guard takes short steps, aims his head at the midriff of the Defensive Lineman, breaking his momentum, whilst the Tackle, breaks down into the side of the Defensive man, preventing any roll out.

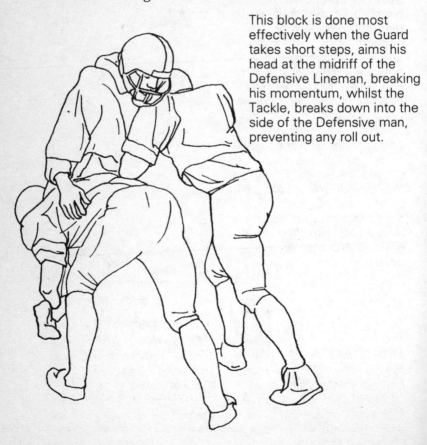

Pass block

Success at the pass block depends on the Defensive Lineman's pass rush being stopped by a hard, stunning first strike.

Once the Defensive Lineman's first momentum has been broken, the blocker can fend off his opponent, using outstretched arms and open hands. He must not however use his hands to grasp his opponent or push him from behind. An important factor in successful pass blocking is for the Offensive Lineman to have quick and agile feet, enabling him to change direction as he has no idea from where the defenders will attack.

FAULT-FINDER

One of the reasons Defensive players are able to tackle the ball carrier is because the block has not been maintained. In other words not only is the first contact important but follow-through with quick, short driving steps is imperative to ensure the success of the block. Remember that if the blocker powers out without control, he will be over extended and easily shedded by his opponent and he will have failed in his duties of run block, protection.

Split End/Tight End

Both the Split End and the Tight End can be used in block protection So the above descriptions will also apply to them. But they are both used for receiving, and so must be able to catch the ball correctly. Often their role is to take short, quick passes in traffic, that is where Defensive coverage is most likely to be used. Their ability to catch and hold on to the ball is all important.

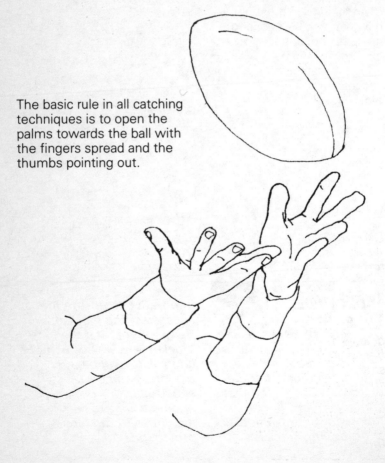

The basic rule in all catching techniques is to open the palms towards the ball with the fingers spread and the thumbs pointing out.

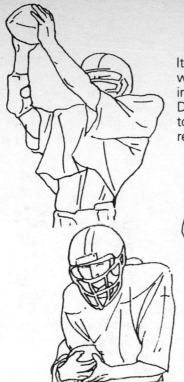

It is imperative that the receiver watches the ball all the way into his hands ignoring the Defensive tackle that is going to follow, once he has received the ball.

LAW-BREAKER
A catch completed following a valid fair catch signal (receiving player raises one arm in the air) is a fair catch. The kicked ball is considered dead where the ball has been caught and the catcher should not be tackled, nor should he run with the ball. The catch is invalid if the catcher signals after the catch or if he then runs with the ball.

THE REFEREE'S DECISION
Invalid fair catch signal
Penalty – 15 yards

LAW-BREAKER

Offensive pass interference, rule relates snapping and passing of the ball.
A potential Offensive eligible receiver is not allowed to make contact with his opponent in an effort to prevent his opponent from intercepting the ball, whilst the ball is in the air.
It is not considered Offensive pass interference when immediately following the snap, the Offensive player charges and makes contact with his opponent at a point not more than one yard beyond the neutral zone and that contact does not continue for more than 3 yards. The Offensive receiver is also allowed to make contact with his opponent as long as he is making a bona fide attempt to reach, catch or bat the pass. An eligible

receiver has an equal right to the ball as a Defensive player.

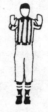 

THE REFEREE'S DECISION
Pass interference
Penalty — 15 yards
Loss of down

LAW-BREAKER
No member of the team in possession may bat the ball forward in an attempt to gain further yardage.

THE REFEREE'S DECISION
Ball illegally kicked
Loss of down

The Quarterback

As we all know the Quarterback is the passer of the Offensive team and so it is important that his technique is correct if that pass is going to be successful.

As soon as he receives the ball from the Center, he must spread his hand out as much as possible, gripping the ball towards its end with his index finger pointing backwards and his third and fourth fingers pointing across the lace.

LAW-BREAKER
If a snap has been proceeded by a huddle or a shift all players of the Offensive team must come to an absolute stop and stay stationary in their position for at least 1 full second before the ball has been snapped.

THE REFEREE'S DECISION
Illegal motion
Penalty — 5 yards

The throwing action is similar to that of throwing a javelin. The Quarterback will look towards the potential receiver before throwing the ball. His arm will follow a line almost parallel to his body, with his elbow cocked as the ball moves forward. He will straighten his arm, as the ball moves over his head.

Potentially, this is the most crucial point, as it is the point of release. If release is too early or too late, then it is likely that the pass will be unsuccessful.

LAW-BREAKER

No player offensively or defensively may bat a loose ball in the direction of their play if the ball is in the field of play, or in any direction if they are in the end zone. However while a forward pass is in flight any player eligible to touch the ball may bat it in any direction and any defensive player may block or partially block a scrimmage kick either in the field of play or in the end zone.

THE REFEREE'S DECISION

Unsportsmanlike conduct
Penalty — 15 yards

On release, the Quarterback must follow through, with his arm pointing in the direction of the ball's intended line. With that momentum, the ball will speed toward its intended target.

On release the Quarterback will spin his hand to the inside and the ball is propelled with the forward movement of the arm and the inside movement of the hand. This creates the famous spiral effect.

LAW-BREAKER
A forward pass is illegal when an inelegible receiving Offensive player touches the ball before an opponent has touched it.

THE REFEREE'S DECISION
Ball illegally touched, kicked or batted
Loss of down

LAW-BREAKER
A forward pass is illegal when an Offensive ineligible receiver has passed the line of scrimmage, before the forward pass has been thrown, however there are exceptions to this rule, i) an Offensive player may charge into his opponent and drive him back no more than 3 yards from the neutral zone, provided that contact was made no more than 1 yard beyond the neutral zone. ii) when an Offensive player who has driven an opponent back 3 yards and has lost contact stays stationary at that spot until after the ball has been thrown.

THE REFEREE'S DECISION
Ineligible Receiver downfield
Loss of down

The Handoff

In addition to throwing the ball, the handoff from the Quarterback to his Running Backs is just as crucial. It is he who must put the ball into the hands of the ball carrier. The ball carrier should be looking for gaps into which to run and not at the ball. The manner in which the Quarterback puts the ball into the hands of the ball carrier is therefore all important. It must be done with a firm and fast action ensuring a fumble is unlikely.

The Flankerback/Wide Receiver

As indicated by their roles, the primary responsibility of these players is pass reception. Therefore their ability to catch the ball is of paramount importance. One of the factors that helps a receiver to be able to catch the ball on the run, just before he is likely to be tackled, is hand to eye co-ordination. The ability to ignore everything going on around him and concentrate totally on catching is a very difficult skill. Like their Offensive colleagues who have a variety of different blocking techniques, the Flankerback/Wide Receiver and indeed, Split End and Tight End have different techniques for the different catches to be made.

LAW-BREAKER

Team mates of the ball carrier shall not grasp, push, lift or run into him in an attempt to assist his forward progress. a) the ball carrier himself shall not grasp or jump on to the back of a team mate in an attempt to gain further yardage. b) team mates of the ball carrier or passer may legally block for him but may not use interlocked interference by grasping one another in a manner to prevent an opponent contacting the player.

THE REFEREE'S DECISION

Interlocking, interference, pushing or helping the runner
Penalty — 5 yards

Waist-high catches
If the ball is thrown and is to be received at waist-level, the receiver should open his palms towards the ball, with his fingers pointing down and his thumbs pointing out. Here a relaxed posture is needed as it is easy for the ball to 'pop out'.

The high ball
When attempting to catch the ball high, the receiver will probably have to jump, which will, of course, leave him vulnerable to being hit or attacked in mid-air. Therefore his concentration is all important.

When a pass is thrown above the height of the receiver's chest, he must point his fingers upwards, with thumbs turned in, so that the ball can be caught and then dragged down towards his chest to ensure a safe catch is completed.

The low catch

The low throw requires the receiver to sometimes go into a crouching position.

Scooping up the ball requires a straight back, keeping the body behind the ball. The idea here is that if the ball is mis-handled, it shouldn't pop-out into the hands of the waiting defender. He should point his fingers downwards with thumbs pointing out for reception.

The over the shoulder pass reception

Probably the most difficult pass reception for a receiver to make, is the over the shoulder pass reception. This is the play which excites the crowds the most, as it involves the Quarterback throwing a 'long bomb' to a receiver who is in full stride, a good distance away from him. The receiver needs to maintain perfect concentration as the ball is speeding to him over his shoulder into his outstretched hands, whilst he is sprinting at full speed. Good hand to eye co-ordination is therefore essential on this play for success.

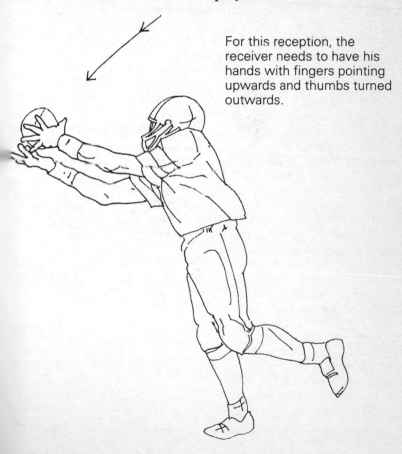

For this reception, the receiver needs to have his hands with fingers pointing upwards and thumbs turned outwards.

Running Backs (Fullback/Tailback)

Every Running Back has his own natural way of running; some shuffle their feet, whilst others pick their knees up in a pumping, driving action. For obvious reasons the latter will always have the advantage. All good Running Backs need to have quick feet and neither foot should be on the ground for longer than it takes to push off, maintaining the player's momentum. One very great technique that a Running Back acquires is to make himself as compact as possible as he is about to be tackled, for by doing this he saves himself unnecessary punishment. Yet in making himself more compact he acquires the ability to inflict it on his opponent. As the saying goes 'it is much better to give than to receive'.

LAW-BREAKER

No player shall run into or throw himself against an opponent who is obviously out of the play, either before or after the ball has been called dead.
No player shall grasp the facemask or helmet opening of an opponent. The open hand may be legally used on the mask but not when grasped.
No player shall intentionally use his helmet to ram an opponent. No player should attempt to spear an opponent. No player should intentionally attempt to strike a runner with his helmet.

THE REFEREE'S DECISION

Personal foul
Penalty — 15 yards
Loss of down

The Running Back's stance is similar to that of his Offensive Linemen in that he uses a three point stance.

The stance

He should position his feet straight ahead and parallel to the line of scrimmage, with the toes of his back foot opposite to the arch of his front foot. Like his Offensive Linemen, his weight should be balanced on the balls of his feet, with his fingers lightly touching the ground, hence giving the power to his legs. He should square his shoulders with his back parallel to the ground. His head should be up and eyes looking straight ahead. The Running Back can disguise where he is going to run.

Upon receiving the handoff from the Quarterback he should have his inside arm down, with his hand pointing upwards and his parallel, outside arm above, with his fingers pointing downwards. This leaves a gap between the two, where the Quarterback is going to place the ball. The Running Back should be looking straight ahead, looking for potential gaps and not looking downwards for the ball. As mentioned earlier, it is the Quarterback's responsibility to place the ball into the Running Back's stomach, so all the Running Back should do is keep his eyes on the gap to which he is running.

Cougars versus Lions

An imaginary offensive drive
The ideal objective of the offensive drive is a
Touchdown but if this cannot be achieved they want to
score at least a Field Goal. As mentioned earlier, a drive
is rarely completed in a single play, and therefore the
Offense has to move the ball towards the opponents'
end zone, through a series of running and passing
plays. The Offense should control the football by
making First downs, ensuring that they maintain
possession and continue their drive. On receiving the
ball the Offense has four downs to make ten yards.
Incidentally, first downs have nothing to do with the
ten yard increments that are marked on the football
field. The downs are measured by the chain marker
and the down marker. The ten yard increments are
there to indicate the position of the Offensive team on
the field at any one time.

Cougars versus Lions
For reference in this imaginary play, the Offense is
called the Cougars and the Defense the Lions.
    The Cougars take possession of the football at their
own 20 yards line following a turnover of possession
from a fumble. So the position of the ball as they
commence the drive, is at their own 20 yards line and
at 1st down and 10.
    On 1st down, the Cougars' Fullback carries the ball
through the middle for a 3 yard gain. After the referee
has spotted the ball at that position, the down marker
will move to a spot laterally to the ball, on the sideline
and change his marker to 2nd down. This now
indicates to everyone both on and off the field, that the
down situation is 2nd down and 7 yards to go.
    On 2nd down, the Quarterback passes the ball to the
Tight End, who after catching the ball is tackled for a 5

Four Offensive Plays

Key
→ Direction of run
⊢ Motion of player to blocking position
× 'Hand off' of ball
—·—·— Passing play
— — — — Direction of Ball Carrier

1. OFF TACKLE RUN

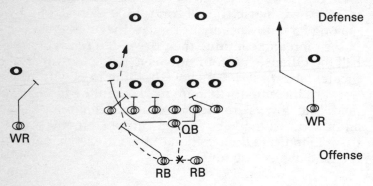

2. SWEEP

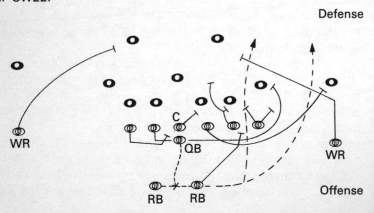

3. MISDIRECTION/COUNTER PLAY

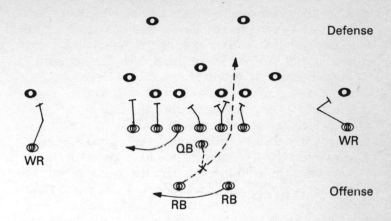

4. PASSING PLAYS/OPTIONS

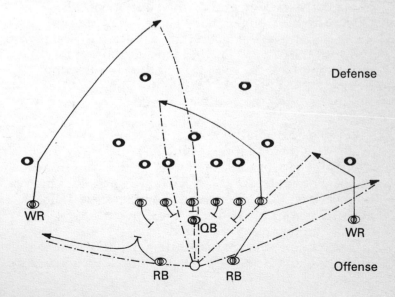

yard gain. Once again the referee spots the ball at the completion of the play and indicates that the down marker should move to this position, indicating 3rd down and 2 yards to go. This is a critical down for the Cougars, for failure to make the necessary yardage to make First down will leave them with the decision on 4th down, either to attempt to gain the necessary yardage and perhaps turn the ball over to the opposition if they fail, or to punt the ball away by kicking it as far down the field into the opposition's territory as possible and maybe give up possession.

However, the Cougars decide to once again use their Powerback, their Fullback to run the ball through the middle and again he gains 3 yards. This means that in three plays, the Cougars have gained 11 yards, one yard more than the necessary yardage to gain their next First down. So the Cougars continue their possession of the ball, once again starting at First down and 10, this time from their own 31 yard line.

On this play, the Cougars' Quarterback rolls out and throws a 32 yard bomb to the Wide Receiver, who is immediately tackled and pushed out of bounds. Obviously the Cougars have gained the 10 yards necessary and so yet again they will start at First down and 10 at the 37 yard line in Lions' territory. Once the chain gang have moved into position and the down marker has set his mark to one, the Cougars commence their drive at First and 10 at the Lions' 37 yard line.

On this occasion the Cougars attempt a sweep right, with their Tailback as the ball carrier. Unfortunately for him, the Lions' Defensive End reads the play accurately and tackles him 3 yards into his own backfield. In other words he tackles the Tailback at the Lions' 40 yard line. So the Cougars are faced with a 2nd down and 13 situation.

On this play, the Cougars attempt a flare pass to the Tailback who catches the ball in his back field 3 yards

again behind the line of scrimmage. However, the
Offensive line has blocked well, and he runs and
dodges his tackles for a gain of 9 yards. The referee
marks the ball and the down marker sets his marker to
3. The Cougars are in a situation of 3rd down and 4, at
the Lions' 31 yard line.

Now the Cougars' Quarterback rolls out and throws
a pass to his Wide Receiver, on the right hand side for
a 12 yard gain. This gives them First down possession
and they will begin their next series of plays from the
Lions' 19 yard line. However, on First down and 10,
the Cougars fool the Lion's Defense by pulling a draw
play. This is where they fake a pass and then the
Quarterback hands the ball to the Tailback, who then
runs through the middle of the gaps that have been
created for him by his Linemen. The Cougars' Tailback
runs straight through and scores Touchdown.

This completes the imaginary play. Here of course it
was successful, not all drives are successful and can
result in incompletions, dropped passes, fumbles and
at worst turnover of possession to the opposition.

The Half Back Option Pass See keys – pages 16/42

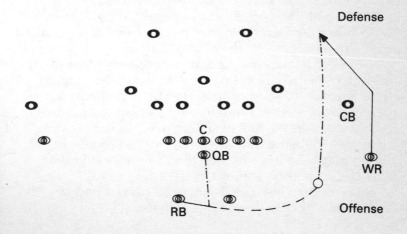

The Defense

The Defensive Unit's Objective

The objective of the Defensive unit is to prevent the opponent's Offense from scoring and keeping possession of the ball for too long. The Defense want to get the ball back for their Offense to get a chance to score. But the Defense can also score for their own team. They can return an interception for a Touchdown, they can return a fumble for a Touchdown and they can cause a Safety by tackling an Offensive ball carrier in his own end zone.

However the main objective of the Defense is to stop the opposing Offense from making first downs, forcing them to 'punt' the ball so that their Offense can get possession of the football and hopefully score. Unlike the Offense the Defensive unit has no rules controlling what sort of alignment they have to make.

The Defense can have as many men on the line of scrimmage as they like. But they have to bear in mind that their men have to combat the run and the passing game of the Offense. Therefore by placing too many or too few men on the line of scrimmage, there is always the danger of being outnumbered by the Offense in certain plays. Because of this, the Defensive unit will usually decide their alignment according to the position on the field, the down to be played and of course the formation set by the Offense.

The Roles of the Defensive Players

Defensive Linemen/Tackles and Ends

It is the mission of the Defensive Linemen to control the line of scrimmage. They must be able to defend themselves from the charge of their Offensive opponents and not be driven back off the line of scrimmage. It has been said many times that the team which controls the line of scrimmage, wins the game.

The aim of the Defensive End is to contain the play to his inside. He will always bring the ball carrier back in to his Defensive line team mates. The physical characteristics of the Defensive Linemen are size, strength, speed and body balance. These are essential, if he is to avoid being blocked and if he is to shed his Offensive opponents, to get to the ball carrier.

The Linebacker

Every position on the Defensive unit is important, but the role of the Linebacker is of paramount importance, if the unit is to function effectively. The Linebacker is the Defensive counterpart of the Quarterback on the Offensive unit. He is their general. It is his responsibility not only to support the Defensive Linemen, but also to help cover for the Defensive backs. He is expected to take on the Offensive Lineman who is attempting to block him, then shed him and help make the Defensive tackle on the ball carrier.

He is also expected to drop back on a passing situation and help cover potential receivers. The characteristics of a Linebacker are that he must be strong enough to cope with and defeat the blocks of Offensive Linemen, and yet quick and mobile enough to cover against Pass Receivers. He must also be intelligent enough to read the Offensive sets and cover quickly and accurately. All-in-all the Linebacker is the Defensive all-rounder and it requires superb all round athletic ability to play this position.

The Defensive Secondary
Cornerbacks and Safeties
The primary responsibility of the Defensive Secondary is to defend against the pass. However, when the opposition is running the ball, they must defend against that as well. Because of this, the Defensive Secondary player must possess great athletic ability. His characteristics are that he must be fast enough to be able to prevent the speedy Wide Receivers from getting beyond him on passing plays, yet tough and strong enough to tackle the most powerful Running Backs.

Defensive Techniques

Linemen/Tackles/Ends
The first and most important technique that the Defensive Lineman must learn is to fight through the pressure of the Offensive Lineman's block. He must assess which way the Offensive Lineman is trying to block him and must fight against that pressure. It is obvious that the Offensive Lineman is trying to protect the area behind him, to enable the ball carrier to run unhindered. If the Defensive Lineman goes around and with the pressure, he will find he has taken himself out of the play, since he will now be behind the ball.

The Nose Tackle
The Nose Tackle aligns opposite the Offensive Center. His basic assignment is to charge at and defeat the Center, preventing him from blocking and protecting the ball carrier. One technique used is to crowd the

ball, especially if he is bigger and stronger than the Offensive Center. However if he is not bigger and stronger, he should drop back from the line of scrimmage and give himself time to read the movement of the Guards and Running Backs.

In order to prevent the Center from blocking him to either side the Nose Tackle should step in with his back foot, bringing it parallel with his front foot, as it was in his original stance. He raises his hand into the Center, forcing him back. By keeping his shoulders and feet parallel, the Nose Tackle should effectively be able to block the Center's block to the left or to the right.

The other Defensive Tackles' techniques are similar to the Nose Tackle's, in that at the snap of the ball they should penetrate the Offensive line hitting their opponents with their inside shoulders, keeping their heads up, watching the position of the ball.

If he penetrates the gap of the Offensive Guards he should try to stay on his feet, searching for the ball carrier and pursuing him.

LAW-BREAKER

A Defensive player may not make contact or impede his opponent in an attempt to prevent him from making a legal reception of the ball whilst the ball is in the air. It is not considered Defensive pass interference when immediately following the snap, the defending player makes contact with his opponent at a point that is one yard beyond the neutral zone or, as in the case of the Offensive receiver if the defending player is making a bona fide attempt to reach, catch or bash the pass.

THE REFEREE'S DECISION

Defensive pass interference Automatic first down

FAULT-FINDER

Although it is important to pursue the ball carrier or Quarterback, whoever is in possession, the Defensive Tackles should not forget that their first responsibilty is to secure their area, before they leave it to pursue the football.

The Defensive Ends have a different technique, generally having a different stance to begin with. One technique is to never go deeper into the Offensive line than the position of the ball. He should try always to keep the ball at least 1-2 yards deeper in the back field than his own position. This will enable him to meet the blocker and move the ball, regardless of whether the ball carrier tries to run inside or outside his position.

Containment is his prime responsibility and the Defensive End should aim either to make the tackle to the inside, or force the ball carrier out of bounds, before the line of scrimmage. By using the side line the Defensive End is again using a special technique of containment. If the ball should move away from him, he must pursue it across the line of scrimmage until he is as deep as the ball carrier. Having achieved this depth in the back field, he should pursue, keeping his balance and keeping control. So that should the Offensive team reverse the direction of play, he will be in a position to counter it. If the Quarterback drops back to pass, then it is generally the Defensive End's responsibilty to rush as quickly as possible to the Quarterback and try to tackle him. However, he must always make sure that a potential pass receiver is not drifting out into his area first. Many Quarterbacks use this tactic to draw Defensive Ends out of position to gain yardage. It is therefore vital that the Defensive End learns the technique of looking before acting.

The stance
The stance of Defensive Lineman depends on whether you are a Tackle or an End

Tackle
There are two standard stances for the Defensive Tackles, the three point stance and the four point stance. Other than the position of the hands the stances are identical.

LAW-BREAKER
Defensive players are prohibited from blocking an eligible Offensive receiver below the waist unless attempting to get at the ball or ball carrier. a) all players are prohibited from blocking below the waist except against the ball carrier during a free kick or scrimmage kick situation. b) all players are prohibited from blocking below the waist except against the ball carrier when a change of possession has occurred. c) an Offensive player in position to receive a backward pass and behind the neutral zone shall not be blocked below the waist.

THE REFEREE'S DECISION
Illegal blocking below the waist
Penalty — 15 yards

The Tackle stands with feet, shoulder-width apart, knees bent and legs coiled. His hips should be slightly lower than his shoulders, leaning forward with the minimum of weight on his hand or hands.

It is this position which gives the Defensive Lineman the power to blast forward and attack his Offensive opponents. He is like a sprinter, poised and ready to blast off at the snap of the ball.

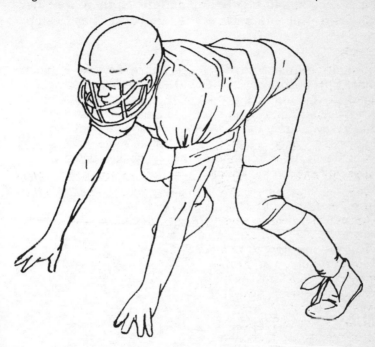

FAULT-FINDER

It is always important not to lean forward on to your hands in the stance, as this immediately disturbs your balance. If you lean back, sitting on your haunches, it will be difficult to power forward easily.

The Linebacker

The Linebacker will often key on an Offensive Lineman who is not covered by his own Defensive Linemen, or on the movement of the Running Backs. These movements will often dictate the Linebacker's reactions. He has a wide range of responsibilites. Firstly, he has to secure the 'middle'. If the Offensive play is run up the middle, the Linebacker has to step

He should drive at a point just off the hip of the Offensive blocker so that he is not vulnerable to being trapped away from the ball carrier. His stance is a two point stance, bent from the hips and flexed in the knees.

He has to stay low, in order to attack the much bigger Offensive Lineman. If he is caught standing up he is a much bigger target and therefore more vulnerable to being knocked down.

LAW-BREAKER
Defensive players shall not
deliberately impede an
eligible receiver from
potentially catching the
ball. When there is doubt
over the situation a legal
forward pass is considered
catchable. If Defensive pass
interference is called the
Offensive team is given
possession at the spot of
the foul and first down.

THE REFEREE'S DECISION
Pass interference
Automatic first down

forward, towards the line of scrimmage and attack the
Offensive Linemen using his regular block protection
technique.

On occasions the Quarterback moves in different
directions from the snap, in an attempt to throw off
the Linebacker's pursuit. So the Linebacker will also
key on the movements of the Running Backs. He
should always read the nearest back to him. If it is a
drive play, he should always step up to the line of
scrimmage, taking on the blockers and hoping to make
the tackle. If the play is a sweep (a play which is run
to the outside of the field or which is run just outside
the Offensive Tackle or Tight Ends) the Linebacker has
to pursue the ball laterally, not up field but around the
end, and then make the tackle. If he is not low and
does not make the proper lateral movement, he is
more vulnerable to being knocked down by the
Offensive Guard. The Linebacker is responsible for
dropping back to help cover against the Offensive
pass.

In this instance he must cover his zone or assigned man, until the ball is in the air. Then he can move quickly to the ball and help once again to make the tackle. On occasion, in an attempt to confuse the Offensive team's blocking positions, the Linebacker will move positions before the snap.

The most common snap is in co-ordination with a Defensive Lineman or Defensive End. The plan is to have the Linebacker penetrate the line of scrimmage and rush the passer and try to force the play for a loss, by tackling the ball carrier behind the line of scrimmage. Once the Linebacker has penetrated the line, he must seek the ball and move to it. He is often the team's top tackle, he therefore needs to perfect his techniques for tackling the ball carrier. Depending on the position of the ball carrier the specific technique will vary. One technique is to knock the ball carrier out of bounds.

LAW-BREAKER
Defensive players can use their hands and arms to push, pull, grasp, lift and twist their opponents in an attempt to reach the ball carrier. They must not however use their hands and arms to tackle an opponent other than the ball carrier. If no attempt is being made to get to the ball carrier the defending player must comply with the above.

THE REFEREE'S DECISION
Illegal use of hands, arms or body
Penalty — 10 yards

LAW-BREAKER
"Any act of unnecessary roughness is considered a personal foul". No player shall kick or strike an opponent with the knee, nor should he strike an opponent's head, neck or face using his forearm, elbow, locked hands, palm, fist or attempt to gouge at an opponent, either during the game or between periods.

THE REFEREE'S DECISION
Personal foul
Loss of down
Penalty — 15 yards

Keeping his head up and neck pulled in towards his shoulders, he keeps his buttocks low, grabbing with both arms around his opponent's waist or thighs. He drives with his legs, maintaining the attack until the ball carrier is down and stopped. Without doubt it is the most impotrtant skill and technique the Linebacker will learn.

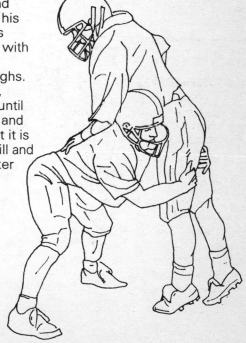

The Defensive Secondary
Cornerbacks and Safeties

The fundamental technique of the Cornerbacks and Safeties remains the same, regardless of how their Defensive unit aligns.

The stance

Their stance should be similar to the Linebacker, but with a slightly more upright position because of the danger of being blocked by an Offensive Lineman.

Standing with his feet shoulder-width apart, knees slightly bent and one foot dropped slightly back, the Cornerback or Safety should be able to move quickly and in any direction.

All Defensive Secondary players must automatically defend against pass coverage first and must continue to do so until they are certain that the play is not a pass. Only then, should they consider leaving their assignment and attacking the ball carrier. Many of their opponent Wide Receivers run excellent pass patterns, making it extremely difficult for the Cornerback to defend, so the Cornerback may adopt the 'bump and run' technique to counter this. This is designed to give the Cornerback time to defend against the pass. It enables him to stay with the Receiver and not be 'burned'.

LAW-BREAKER
Once the ball has been called ready for play and until it has been snapped no Defensive player may touch the ball unless it has been moved illegally. No Defensive player may contact an opponent unless he has, again, moved illegally. No Defensive player may be in or beyond the neutral zone at the snap. No Defensive player may call Defensive signals that simulate the sound of the Offensive snap or shall use words or signals that disturb the Offensive team.

THE REFEREE'S DECISION
False start, illegal motion
Penalty – 5 yards

THE REFEREE'S DECISION
Offside or encroachment
Penalty – 5 yards

To play the 'bump and run', the Cornerback should line up on the inside shoulder of the Receiver, about 1-2 yards from him. As the ball is snapped the defender will then step into the Receiver, hit him and delay his release and so delay his pass pattern.

However he must release the Receiver and so will turn and chase him. It is vital therefore that the Cornerback retains coverage of the Receiver. He will watch the Receiver and wait until he looks for the ball, then he will do so too. By maintaining this concentration on the man, rather than waiting for the ball, the Cornerback should maintain good coverage.

LAW-BREAKER
No player shall trip an opponent, ie. he shall not strike an opponent with his foot or any part of his leg that is below the knee.

THE REFEREE'S DECISION
Tripping
Penalty — 10 yards

Under normal pass coverage the Cornerback will take backpedal steps to give a cushion between himself and the Receiver. Once again, he must prevent the Receiver running past him. Allowing the Receiver to get past him opens the game for a potential easy score.

LAW-BREAKER
No player shall tackle or block the runner when he is clearly out of bounds. Nor should he throw him to the ground after the ball has become dead.

THE REFEREE'S DECISION
Personal foul
Penalty — 15 yards
Loss of down

As stated earlier, if the Cornerback is certain that the Offensive play is a run, he must shed his potential blocker and help to make the tackle. He must therefore be as strong in the tackle as the Linebacker and his tackling technique must be as consistent as the Linebacker's too.

The Safeties' responsibilty is the same as the Cornerback's, that is pass coverage. To simplify their assignments they will usually change position, depending on the position of the Offensive team's Tight End. The Safety who aligns opposite the Tight End is called the Strong Safety, whilst the Free Safety has no immediate responsibility for any potential pass receiver.

He is the American Football's equivalent of Soccer's sweeper. He is free to roam the Secondary and give support where it is most needed.

One of the techniques of the two Safeties is that they act and react as a team. If an Offensive play moves to one side or the other, then the Safeties will move to that side, one covering the outside, and the other the

LAW-BREAKER
No defensive player shall charge into the passer when it is obvious that the ball has been thrown.
No player may block the kicker of a free kick until he has advanced 5 yards beyond his restraining line or until the kick has touched a player, an official or the ground. No player should attempt to chop block an opponent.

THE REFEREE'S DECISION
Personal foul
Penalty — 15 yards
Loss of down

inside of the Cornerback, thus giving the Cornerback security should he be beaten by the Offense. Neither of the Safeties concerns himself with run coverage, until he is certain that the ball will not be thrown.

To summarize, as mentioned earlier, tackling is considered the most important technique for a Defensive player. If he is unable to make a good tackle then he is unable to play Defense. It has been said that the perfect tackle is just getting the ball carrier on to the ground. But it is to the Defensive unit's advantage to punish the ball carrier whenever possible. By tackling as hard and as fast, and as aggressively as possible, they will discourage the ball carrier from running the ball so hard.

The perfect tackling technique can be described as pursuing the ball carrier low and hard, keeping the knees flexed just before contact.

The Defender drives his head and shoulder underneath the ball carrier, placing his helmet underneath the ball, hopefully knocking it loose from the ball carrier. He drives his shoulder into the mid-section of the ball carrier all at once. Once he has hit the runner, it is important to wrap his arms around him, maintaining balance. He keeps driving his feet and pushing the ball carrier back.

FAULT-FINDER

Never let the ball carrier drive you forward and so gain more yardage. Sling or drive him to the ground and so discourage him from coming back for more. It is very important to master this technique to stop the Offense, your primary objective. Don't forget that first you have to be able to play off a blocker, before you can make that tackle.

A great deal of time is spent at practice with certain drills for taking on blockers and making the tackle. The Defensive player takes great pride in his ability to make hard and effective tackles and play aggressive football.

LAW-BREAKER
No participating player shall commit a personal foul during the game or between the periods.
No player shall grasp the face mask or helmet opening of an opponent. A 15 yards penalty, as in this case, is imposed for unintentional or incidental grasping of the opponents face mask.

THE REFEREE'S DECISION
Personal foul
Penalty — 15 yards
Loss of down

The Kicking Teams/Special Teams

One of the most important and yet under-rated units of the football team is the Kicking Team. Without exception all of the teams in the NFL will confirm that without a sound kicking game and excellent Special Team unit, the chances of winning the championship are slight.

The Kicking game is a major part of the Offensive arsenal and yet an important part of the Defensive strength. If a side has a good Kicking Team, the Field Goal can be used as a major scoring weapon. Yet with a good Special Team, the ability to defend against the Field Goal, or block an attempt to rush the kicker and so foil the attempt is a major factor in your defensive strategy.

The Special Teams unit on kickoffs and punt returns can turn around a game for that unexpected score. Likewise, the kickoff and punt coverage teams can stop their opponents deep in their own territory and set their Defensive unit up in good field positions.

The Roles of the Special Teams

Kickoff and kickoff return

The kickoff is one of the most exciting moments in a football game, whether it be the opening kickoff or after a team has scored a Touchdown. The Kicker's role is to kick the ball as deep into the opponent's territory as possible, keeping the ball in the air for as long as possible. This enables his team mates to pursue down field, and so tackle the ball carrier as deep into his own territory as possible. On the other hand, the role of the Kick returner is to return the ball as far back up-field as he can, following his lead blockers and protectors.

LAW-BREAKER

A player of the receiving team who is positioned to catch a free kick or a scrimmage kick, must be given the opportunity to catch that kick by the kicking team. Players of the Kicking team must give the catcher 2 yards clearance whilst the ball is in flight. As soon as the ball has been caught or is touched by any player of the receiving team, or if the ball has touched the ground, then the Kicking team players may make contact.

THE REFEREE'S DECISION
Pass interference
Automatic first down

On receiving the kickoff, the blockers are spaced so that they can block their opponents and then form a protective wedge from behind which the runner can emerge. The Center often has the responsibilty of blocking the other team's Kicker and the two Guards either side of him are often responsible for being the first lined up on either side of the Kicker. Often a kickoff return is called either left, right or straight up the middle and it is the role of the blockers to create space for the ball carrier to run.

Kick Return Formation

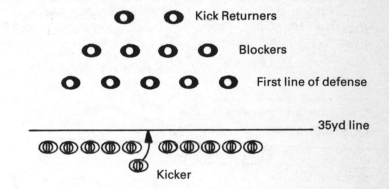

O O Kick Returners

O O O O Blockers

O O O O O First line of defense

_____ 35yd line

Kicker

LAW-BREAKER
The receiving player of a kick or punt shall not carry a caught or recovered ball for more than 2 yards in any direction after a fair catch call has been signalled.

THE REFEREE'S DECISION
Ball illegally touched, kicked or batted
Loss of down

Punt and punt return

The responsibility of the Punter is to get the maximum distance into his punt, especially if he can achieve height with his kick too. This should give time for his team mates to get down-field and contain the Punt returner for no gain.

On the other hand, as with the Kick returner, the Punt return unit is looking to return the ball for as large a gain as possible.

As the punt moves in a high arc and the Defense has time to get down-field, it is almost impossible to return the ball straight down the middle.

Instead, the lead blockers try to create a corridor or screen, so that the runner has time to run between them and the side line. Like the kickoff, the punt is a very exciting moment in the game.

Punting Return Formation

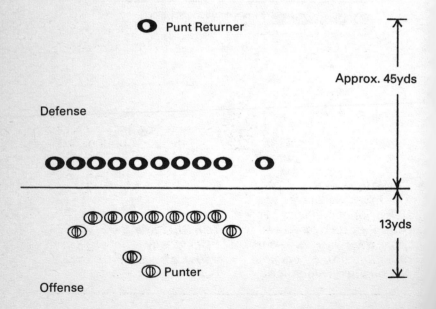

Point after Touchdown/Field Goal unit

The objective of the PAT and Field Goal unit is to give the holder and kicker sufficient time to catch, spot and kick the ball through the uprights for either 1 or 3 points. The Holder will set down on one knee, approximately 7-8 yards from the Center. The Kicker will probably take around 2-3 steps, and has approximately 1.3 seconds from the point of the snap, until his kick to get it safely away.

A good Kicking team is a major part of the Offense's arsenal, however if one play can turn a game around it is the successful blocking of an attempted Field Goal. For this transfers the momentum of the play from one team to the other.

The blocking of Field Goals and Punts, the running back of kickoffs and Punt returns for Touchdowns are all part of the excitement of Special teams. A major contribution to the success of these moments is the individual player's talent, skills and commitment towards making that big play. The Kicking game therefore, as with all other aspects of the game requires concentration and commitment from every player, for every minute, if he is to do his necessary job effectively.

LAW-BREAKER
No player may position himself on the back or shoulders of a team mate prior to the snap in an attempt to gain advantage over the Offensive team. Regarding Field Goal and PAT kicks, no Defensive player may step, jump or stand on a team mate or opponent, be picked up by *a team mate or be lifted by a team mate in an attempt to gain additional height to block a kick.*

THE REFEREE'S DECISION
Unsportsmanlike conduct Penalty — 15 yards

The Techniques of Special Team's Players

The Center

In addition to his responsibility for snapping the ball to the Quarterback during normal playing time, the Center also has to snap the ball for Punts and Field Goals and extra point situations. His technique for snapping the ball long distance is different from his normal technique.

Instead of his feet being positioned slightly one behind the other, as they would be when snapping the ball to the Quarterback, he now has his feet wide apart and parallel to each other. This enables both his elbows to pass freely through his legs, as he makes the powerful snap backwards. The Center grips the ball on the laces with his right hand as a Quarterback would. His left hand is positioned at the back of the ball to guide it. As the ball is centered, it is spun so that it reaches the Kicker spiralling. The ball arrives at waist-height. It is a technique that requires great concentration and practice to perfect.

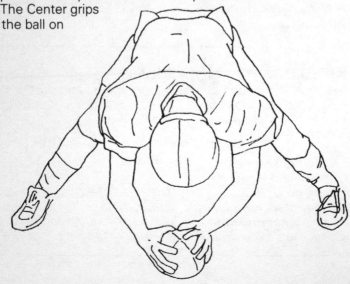

The Punter

One of the primary techniques for a Punter to learn is to ignore a potential rush from the Defense. He has enough to concentrate on, without worrying about other people.

Once the ball is received, the Punter should quickly position the ball in front of and across his body at about hip-level. The heel of the ball should be covered with his palm and his thumb positioned at mid-seam. All of this needs to be done quickly, as the Punter has no more than around 2.3 seconds in which to get the ball away.

The drop is a most important phase of the punt and is controlled by the release. The number of steps the Punter may take will vary, but it is usually about 3.

Contact with the ball should be made at around knee-height and advantage should be taken of strong tail winds, by punting especially high. If the punt is properly executed then the sound of a deep thud and a good spiral ,are the obvious signs to the crowd.

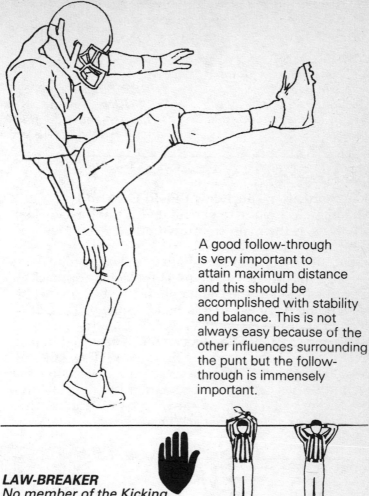

A good follow-through is very important to attain maximum distance and this should be accomplished with stability and balance. This is not always easy because of the other influences surrounding the punt but the follow-through is immensely important.

LAW-BREAKER
No member of the Kicking team shall tackle or block an opponent who has completed a fair catch. Only the player making the fair catch signal has this protection.

THE REFEREE'S DECISION
Personal foul
Penalty – 15 yards
Loss of down

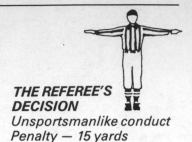

LAW-BREAKER
A Kicker, Holder or Punter who simulates being roughed or run into by a Defensive player commits an unfair act.

THE REFEREE'S DECISION
Unsportsmanlike conduct Penalty — 15 yards

The Point after Touchdown/Field Goal unit

The main technique to perfect on PAT and Field Goal attempts, is the main co-ordination between the Center, Holder and Kicker.

Because the Kicker has about 2 or 3 steps to make before he kicks the ball he must make his approach almost as soon as the Center snaps the ball. In fact his run should be timed so that he kicks the ball a split second after the Holder has placed it ready. If all goes to plan, a snap, hold and kick will be achieved in just over a second and either 1 point on a PAT or 3 points on a Field Goal will have been scored. The Center snap technique has been described earlier but the Holder for the Kicker will have good catching hands and is often a Quarterback, Defensive Back or Receiver.

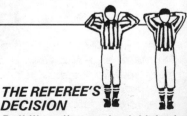

LAW-BREAKER
A kick is illegal when a) a player kicks the ball during a down. b) when a kick returner kicks the ball instead of catching it.

THE REFEREE'S DECISION
Ball illegally touched, kicked or batted Loss of down

If the Kicker is right-footed, the Holder will line up with his left knee on the ground, opposite the spot from which the Kicker is going to make contact. He will then place his fingertips on the ground, on the spot where he intends to place the ball. This gives the Kicker a target for his approach. The Holder will then extend his right hand towards the Center, giving him a target to shoot at. The Center will then snap the ball directly to the Holder's hand.

As soon as the holder receives the ball, he should position it immediately, ready for the kick to be completed. The Holder will then try to ensure that the laces are positioned away from the Kicker, directly in line with the posts. The position of the laces can affect the flight of the ball once kicked.

The ball should be held lightly by the Holder's index finger with just enough pressure to keep the ball upright. It should not be pressed into the ground as this can affect the flight of the ball.

Almost all Kickers now kick the ball soccer-style, contacting the ball with the instep of the foot. As with punting, the follow-through is all important, taking the kicking leg as far through as possible, with the Kicker's eyes still looking where the ball was placed.

American Footballer's Phrasebook

General Terminology

Adjustments
Slight movement sometimes made by the Offensive or
Defensive players after the down and before the snap.
Adjustments are also made after the snap by the
Quarterback and Receiver.

All American
Voted best college player at his specific position by
American Sports' Writers.

All pro
Voted the best NFL player at his specific position by
American Sports' Writers.

Back field
The name given to the area behind the line of
scrimmage.

Back up
A player who does not start the game. He will often
come into the game later, replacing one of the starting
players.

Blind side
The area which is 'Blind' to Quarterbacks using the sprint back technique to pass, it is the area behind him. For example, left-handed passers have a blind side to their right.

Blind snap
This is when the Center has to snap the ball back through his legs a short distance, without being able to see his target, usually the Quarterback on shotgun plays.

Block
A legitimate, intentional obstruction of an opposing player.

Burned
When a Defensive Back has been easily out run by a Receiver, for a long gain.

Carry
Offensive control of the ball by a running play.

Clipping
An illegal block, made by throwing the body across the back of an opponent.

Clutch
A reference made to a successful, difficult pass reception.

Co-ordinator
A member of the coaching staff who takes responsibility for certain aspects of play. For example, a Defensive co-ordinator.

Cut
A reference made to a quick and often deceptive side step made by a ball carrier, usually a Running Back.

Deep zones
A reference given to the zone covered by the Safeties, that will start approximately fifteen yards from the line of scrimmage and will extend to the goal line.

Down situation
This refers to the state of play during the particular Offensive drive, e.g. second down and nine.

Down
The beginning of play, from a set piece from the line of scrimmage.

Drive
This refers to the Offensive team gaining significant yardage during a number of successful plays.

Drop
The distance from the centre, to which a Quarterback would retreat before preparing to pass.

Encroachment
A penalty called on a Defensive player positioned in the neutral zone at the time of the snap, or a Defensive player who makes contact with an opponent before the ball is snapped.

Fake
The action taken by the Offensive team in an attempt to fool the Defensive team. Often a 'fake' is made by the Quarterback who will pretend to hand the ball off and will then pass to a Receiver.

Field Goal
This is a successful place kick from scrimmage and between the hashmarks, worth three points .

Flag
A yellow duster thrown by a referee while a play is in progress, to indicate an infringement has occurred.

Flat
This is the area wide of the hashmarks and behind the line of scrimmage.

Formation
The specific way a team lines up.

Franchise
Presently numbered at 28 teams; a franchise is an individual team granted membership by and of the National Football League.

Free agent
A player who is free to sign for any team – can be a college player not chosen during the draft, or a pro player whose present contract has expired.

Free ball
A ball that can be legally recovered by either side.

Fumble
Usually an Offensive error, it is a dropped or mishandled ball that can be recovered and advanced by any player on the field. A fumble could also be made by a Defensive player who had just intercepted a pass.

Game plan
The Offensive and Defensive teams' tactics chosen before each game.

Huddle
The gathering of players to organise the next play, Defensive or Offensive.

Injured reserve
Refers to a member of the team not listed on the roster.

Line of scrimmage
An imaginary line from where that play begins and which is the width of the field.

Mis-match
This refers to when ill-suited defenders are drawn to cover Offensive Receivers.

Miscue
Any mistake made during the execution of a play, it usually refers to a snap that has failed to be collected by the Quarterback.

Neutral zone
The space between the Offensive and Defensive lines; its width is the length of the ball.

Option
The choice given to Offensive players once play has started.

Pattern or route
The pre-determined course or direction taken by a Receiver.

Penetration
The access gained by a Defensive Lineman across a line of scrimmage into the back field.

Piling on
A penalty called when players intentionally fall or charge into the ball carrier, or any other player on the floor; penalty will result in fifteen yards.

LAW-BREAKER

The Offensive team requirements for a scrimmage are as follows: a) the Center must not move himself or the ball prior to the snap, once he has assumed his position for that play. b) once the ball has been called ready for play by the referee, all Offensive team players must be within 15 yards of the ball. c) before the snap once the Center has touched the ball no player of the Offensive team shall make a false start or be in or beyond the neutral zone (a false start includes i) a shift or movement of an Offensive player that simulates the beginning of play. ii) an Offensive Lineman after having placed his hands on or near to the ground moving his hands or making any quick movement. iii) an Offensive player feigning to charge a Defensive player. iv) false start will not be called if an Offensive player moves when threatened by a Defensive player in the neutral zone. However the threatened Offensive player must not enter the neutral zone. v) at least 7 Offensive players must be set on the line of scrimmage, not less than 5 shall be numbered from 50-79. vi) of the remaining 4 players, one player may be positioned between his scrimmage line and his back field to receive a hand-to-hand snap from the Center. vii) the players directly on either side of the Center may lock legs with that Center. However any other Lineman on Offense must have both feet outside the outside foot of the player next to him when the ball is snapped. viii) all players must be in bounds and not beyond the line of scrimmage. Only the Center may encroach into the neutral zone and even then no part of his body may be beyond the neutral zone and his feet must be stationary behind the ball. ix) one Offensive player may be in motion but not in motion towards his opponents goal line. x) no Offensive Lineman may receive a snap.

THE REFEREE'S DECISION

False start or illegal procedure
Penalty – 5 yards and down repeated

LAW-BREAKER
No player shall deliberately run into a potential receiver when a pass sent to him is obviously not catchable. There shall be no piling on, falling on, jumping on or throwing the body on to an opponent after the ball has been called dead.

THE REFEREE'S DECISION
Personal foul
Penalty — 15 yards
Loss of down

Play book
This contains the team's total strategy, it will list plays, alignments, formations and tactics.

Punt
A kick from the hands, from scrimmage as far into opposition territory as possible, usually resulting in giving up possession. It is a play only undertaken when the Offense does not expect to gain the ten yards required and is playing fourth down.

Rating
This is done on a scale of one to one hundred. It is a comparative assessment of the Quarterback's all round performance.

Reception
A legally caught forward pass, made by an eligible Receiver.

Return
The run back of the ball resulting from an interception, fumble, kick or punt.

Roster
A list of game-eligible players in a team. It has a
maximum of forty five players.

Rookie
A player in his first season.

Roughing the Kicker
A penalty resulting from contact on the Kicker or
Punter, without having previously touched the ball.
The penalty is called for fifteen yards and loss of first
down position.

Running to daylight
A phrase coined by Greenbay's Vince Lombardi,
stressing that Running Backs should look for gaps in
the Defense opening up, if the planned route has been
blocked, and then take such a route to gain extra
yardage.

LAW-BREAKER
*When a kick or punt is
being made no defending
player may run into the
kicker unless the ball has
been touched first. This
rule is split into 2 degrees
of penalty, 5 yards if the
kicker and holder has been
run into and displaced —
but has not been roughed,
15 yards if the kicker and
holder has been
endangered by the
defending player.*

THE REFEREE'S DECISION
*Personal foul
Penalty — 15 yards
Loss of down*

Safety
Worth two points, it is awarded to the defending team
that tackles an Offensive player in possession in his
own end zone.

Safety
Safety also refers to a member of the Offensive
secondary whose role primarily is pass defense, see
Free Safety and Strong Safety.

Scissored
This refers to a ball carrier being tackled from opposite
sides at the same time, one defender hitting low, the
other hitting high.

Scrimmage
This is started by the Center snapping the ball, this
refers to any play.

Seam
The imaginary line between the Linebackers and the
Defensive Backs on zone coverage.

Secondary
The Defensive area covered by the two Cornerbacks
and two Safeties.

Set
The Offensive and Defensive formations immediately
before the snap.

Shift
This refers to any motion on Offense or Defense prior
to the snap. Can be made by an individual or a group
of players.

Shut out
The term given when the opposition has been prevented from scoring.

Side lined
Refers to a player being put out of action, usually by injury.

Snap
This is a backward movement of the ball from the Center to the Quarterback to begin an Offensive play.

Split
The distance between one player and another, usually referred to Linemen.

Spotted
The replacement of the ball made by the referee at the line of scrimmage, once a play has ended.

Starter
A player who begins the game in his position.

Streak
A player's successive performances worthy of note.

Strong Safety
He has the responsibility to cover the Tight End and strongside.

Strongside
The side of the Offensive line on which the Tight End is positioned.

Stutter steps
A term given to the style of fast, short steps used by a ball carrier in an attempt to deceive a defender.

Sudden death
The period of overtime/extra time, if teams were level at full time, the game is decided on first team to score wins.

The plus and minus area
In Offensive terms the field is divided into two sections, the Defense's section- plus, and the Offense's section – minus.

Thirty second clock
This refers to the time allocated to the Offense to commence play from the end of the previous play.

Time out
This refers to when the game clock is stopped at the request of the officials or at the request of a team captain. Each team is allowed three time outs per half.

Touchback
This refers to a kickoff travelling through the back of the end zone or when a Kick Returner or interceptor catches the ball in the end zone and declines to run the ball out, by dropping to one knee. A team in possession will recommence play from the twenty yard line.

Touchdown
Worth six points, a touchdown is gained by either running or passing the ball into the end zone and crossing the plane of the goal line.

Trade
An exchange of either players or draft picks between teams.

Trench or trenches
A term given to the space between the Offensive and
Defensive lines.

Turnovers
This refers to the opposition regaining possession by
way of interceptions or fumble recoveries.

Veteran
A player who has played more than one season in the
NFL.

Wild card team
One of two teams in each conference to qualify for the
play offs with the best won/lost record of non-
divisional winners.

Offensive Terminology

Ace
A name sometimes given to the single back Offense.

Audibles
Play signals call by the Quarterback at the line of
scrimmage, changing the original play which was
called in a huddle.

Ball control Offense
An Offensive tactic to keep possession with running
plays and short passes.

Blockers
Usually Offensive Linemen or Fullbacks who
intentionally and legitimately obstruct their opponents.

Bootleg
A manoeuvre made by the Quarterback in which he fakes to hand the ball off to a Running Back, and will then proceed to run down the field in possession of the ball himself, usually after rolling out towards the side line first.

Button hook
An Offensive Receiver's pattern that begins by heading down field and then suddenly stopping and turning towards the Quarterback, in an attempt to create space from his Defensive marker.

Clear out
An Offensive tactic of luring Defensive Backs from their coverage, by sending Receivers on special routes, with the intention of creating space for a colleague to enter unmarked.

Completion
A successful pass reception made by an eligible Receiver.

Cross pattern
An Offensive Receiver's pattern which is usually used to attempt to lose Defensive backs, it is when 2 Receivers or Tight Ends cross on their patterns, usually around the area of the hashmarks.

Curl
An Offensive pass Receiver's pattern that will take him in a circular motion back towards the Quarterback. A curl pattern can be run either to the outside or to the inside.

Double teaming
An Offensive play made when two Offensive players are used to block one defender.

Draw
An Offensive play created by the Quarterback and
Offensive line faking the passing play, and then
handing the ball late to a Running Back, to enable him
to run straight through the middle. Its description is
taken from drawing Defensive players out of position.

The Draw (split right, 41-draw)   See keys – pages 16/42

Defense

Offense

Dumping off
A quick, short, forward pass made by the Quarterback
to a Running Back, in an effort to evade an
approaching Defensive player.

Flare Pass
A short pass usually made by the Quarterback to a
Running Back.

Flanker
The Wide Receiver positioned on the same side of the
field as the Tight End can also be referred to as a
'Wide Out'.

Flea flicker
An Offensive play made by the Quarterback on a fake run, who will then 'lateral' the ball to a trailing Running Back, just as he is about to be tackled – can also be done by a Receiver after catching the ball, and then 'lateralling' it to a trailing player in an attempt to pick up extra yardage.

Flood
An Offensive play to confuse the Defense by sending a number of Receivers into one area of the field.

Fly or burn pattern
An Offensive pass pattern on which the Receivers will sprint full speed down field.

Fullback or Powerback
Playing the front man in the I formation for Running Backs, usually used for 'blocking' or for powerful runs through the middle to gain a few yards.

Gadget
An Offensive trick play which usually involves changes of direction and occasional passes.

Ground game
This refers to the Offense's running or rushing plays as opposed to passing.

Guard
This is one of two Offensive Linemen who set up either side of the Center.

Halfback
An all-purpose Running Back, who is competent to run, block, catch or pass with equal effectiveness.

Halfback option
An Offensive play, featuring a Running Back's option to either continue his run, or to throw a pass to a Receiver, depending on the Defensive coverage.

Handoff
The Quarterback puts the ball into the hands of a colleague usually a Running Back.

Hook block
Made by an Offensive Lineman, by stepping sideways and then angling the defender away from the ball carrier.

Hurry up Offense
When the Offense ignores 'huddles' and has short snap counts in an attempt to save time.

In pattern
An Offensive Receiver's pass route made by running down field and then cutting towards the inside.

Inbounds running play
An Offensive play intended to keep the ball in play at all costs, it is usually used to waste time during the last two minutes when a team is winning.

Inside running
Offensive running plays directed between the two Offensive Tackles directly up the middle.

Interior line
The Offensive line excluding the Tight End; ie. a Center, two Guards and two Tackles.

Lateral
An underhand pass to another player. It is usually made by the Quarterback to a Running Back, it can be made by a down field player to a trailing player. It can also be referred to as a 'Toss' or 'Pitch Out'.

Long bomb
A very long pass.

Loop
A pass pattern made by a Running Back which will take him from the back field towards the line of scrimmage in a wide arch.

Mis-direction
An Offensive running play aimed at fooling the Defense, by showing one direction and then suddenly shifting to another.

Option run
An Offensive play in which the Quarterback has the option to 'handoff', 'pitch' or continue to run with the ball himself, also see 'Flea Flicker'.

Pass block
A 'block' made by the Offensive Lineman in protection of his Quarterback during a passing play.

Pitch out
See 'lateral'.

Play action
An Offensive passing play which begins with a fake handoff to the Running Back.

Possession pass
A short yardage pass giving almost no chance of interception.

Power sweep
An Offensive running play where both Guards pull from the Offensive line to lead the ball carrier.

Pro-set or 'T' formation
Variations using two Running Backs usually set either side and some distance behind the Quarterback before the snap, (as opposed to in line with the Quarterback as in the I formation).

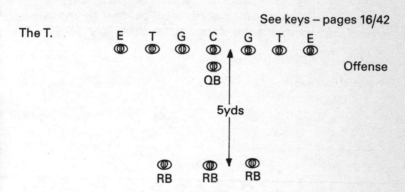

See keys – pages 16/42

The T.

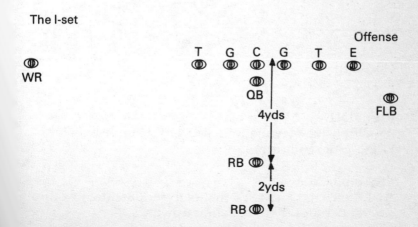

The I-set

Reverse
An Offensive play designed to deceive the Defense by initially showing a run to one direction by way of a sweep, and then handing off, usually to a Receiver, who will return the play in the opposite direction initially behind the Offensive line before turning up field.

Roll out
The Quarterback's motion towards the side line, following his Running Backs as Blockers if he intends to run, or by using the Backs as possible Receivers.

The Roll Out Pass   See keys – pages 16/42

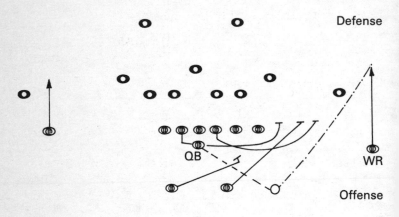

Run block
An Offensive play made to prevent defenders from tackling the ball carrier.

Scoop block
An Offensive Lineman's manoeuvre, pushing low into a defender and then thrusting upwards.

Scramble
A Quarterback trying to avoid a Defensive pass rush by running alone in the back field.

Screen
An Offensive pass play, called when a pass is expected by the Defense. However, after encouraging the Defensive unit to drop back into coverage, the Quarterback will pass short, usually to a Running Back positioned wide in the flat behind his protective Offensive Guard blockers.

Short pass
A forward pass, usually with a completion distance of less than ten yards.

Short passing game
An Offensive strategy, using short, low risk passes to gain yardage, rather than continually running the ball as in 'running game'.

Shotgun
An Offensive formation with the Quarterback set approximately seven yards behind the Center. The formation is usually used to give the Quarterback more time to find an open Receiver during a heavy pass rush.

Single back Offense
An Offensive formation that features only one Running Back in the back field.

Slant
An Offensive running play when the Fullback runs over the Weakside Tackle.

Sneak
A Quarterback running play, designed to gain first down or a touchdown over a short distance.

Split End
The Receiver on the Weakside.

Spot or timing pass
A term given when the Quarterback throws to a particular spot on the field, rather than straight to a Receiver and a timing pass is to the spot on the field where the Receiver should be, having timed his run correctly.

Spread
An Offensive formation with Receivers spread along the line as wide as possible.

Sweep
An Offensive running play, in which the ball carrier will attempt to gain yardage by running in an arching motion, ie. he will run 'laterally' towards the side line before turning upfield.

Swingman
A pre-determined Running Back who will act as a safety valve Receiver, by running wide in the flat.

Tailback
The rear-most Running Back, positioned when the two Running Backs set in line behind the Quarterback.

Trap
An Offensive line manoeuvre, in which a defender is
encouraged to enter a gap in the Offensive line and is
then 'blocked' out of the play.

The Trap See keys – pages 16/42

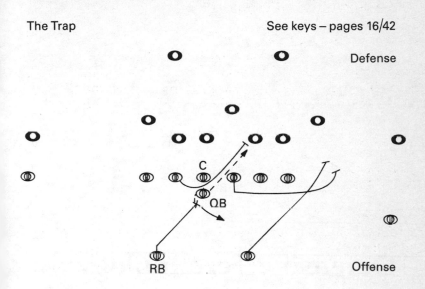

Turning the corner
A Running Back or Receiver's turning up field, after
first heading towards a side line.

Two minute Offense
An Offensive strategy, prepared for the end of a half
or the end of a game. It is usually used when the team
in possession needs to score in a hurry and gain as
much yardage as quickly as possible.

Weakside
The side of the Offensive line without the Tight End.

Wishbone
An Offensive formation, using three Running Backs set in a forward facing triangle, behind the Quarterback.

The Wishbone

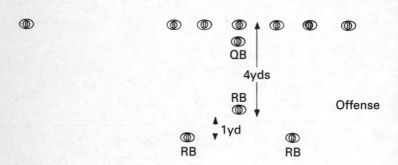

Defensive Terminology

Blanket coverage
Total coverage made by the Defensive Secondary against all eligible pass Receivers.

Blitz
A planned surprise pass rush made by Linebacker/Linebackers, Safety/Safeties or perhaps from both.

Bump and run
A tactic used by the Defensive 'secondary', to affect the route or timing of a Wide Receiver by pushing or shoving that Receiver once, as he sprints out after the snap. This has to occur within 10 yards from the line of scrimmage.

Commit
An action made by a Defensive player who knows he will be out of position, by anticipating an Offensive play if the Offensive play is in any way different from that which he expects.

Containment
A Defensive strategy designed to keep the Offense within itself, ie. preventing the Offense running wide of the defenders.

Cornerback
A Defensive player whose primary responsibility is covering the Offensive Wide Receivers, he is usually one of four Defensive Backs in the secondary.

Coverage
The description given to the efforts made by the Linebackers and Defensive secondary to prevent eligible Receivers from catching passes. It is also a reference given to Defensive formations such as man-to-man and zone coverage.

Deep Back
A reference made to a Defensive Back playing extra deep in the secondary, to cover against the expected pass.

Dime
A Defensive formation which features six Defensive Backs.

Dog
A pass rush made by the Linebackers, either individually or in partnership.

Double coverage
A reference made when one eligible Receiver is covered by either two Defensive Backs, two Linebackers or a combination of both.

Force man
He is a Safety or Cornerback, keeping the Offensive play to the inside or outside, depending on the planned coverage.

Four/threes
A Defensive formation which comprises four Linemen and three Linebackers.

Free Safety
A Defensive Back, responsible for covering middle and deep zones, he has no immediate responsibility for any particular Receiver coming deep, and is free to roam the secondary, giving support where it is most needed.

Front alignment
This refers to the formation of the Defensive line.

Interception
This is when a Defensive player catches a pass intended for an Offensive Receiver.

Key
This is when a Defensive player is able to anticipate the forthcoming Offensive play from the movement or formation of the Offense.

Man-to-man
A Defensive pass formation, ensuring that each eligible Receiver is assigned to a particular man in the Defense, usually involving Linebackers and Defensive secondary.

Man-2 coverage versus twin back offense

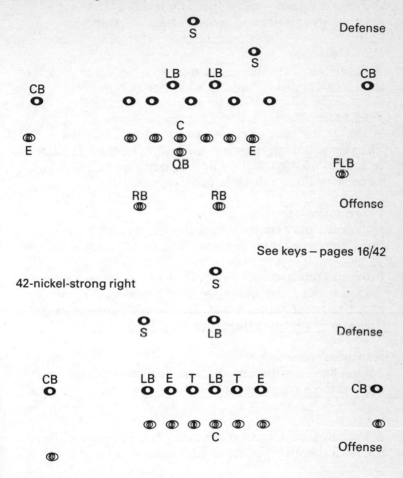

See keys – pages 16/42

42-nickel-strong right

Nickel
A Defensive formation featuring a fifth Defensive
Back, usually acquired by taking out a Linebacker.

Nose Tackle
The central Defensive Lineman in a three or five man
Defensive line, who usually aligns facing the Center.

Overshift
A Defensive ploy, moving its Defensive line to one side, in anticipation of play in that direction.

Pass Defenses
A defensive formation specifically designed to counter the pass, see 'Dime' and 'Nickel' formations.

Pass rush
A Defensive play designed to prevent or hurry a Quarterback from passing the ball, by either sacking him or blocking his pass, It is usually made by the Defensive line or outside Linebackers.

Playing the gap
Defensive play by seeking to fill the spaces between the Offensive Linemen.

Prevent Defense
A Defensive formation specifically designed to prevent major yardage gain. It will allow short yardage gains that take time from the Offense.

Run prevention
A Defensive formation or tactic designed to stop the opposition's running play.

Sack
A tackle of the Quarterback whilst still in possession of the ball, behind the line of scrimmage.

Stack
A Defensive tactic with the Linebacker lining up directly behind his Defensive Lineman, giving no clues to his coverage or pass rush intentions.

Stunt
A planned rush by Defensive Ends and Linebackers by looping around each other, in an effort to penetrate behind the line of scrimmage and tackle the ball carrier for a loss of yardage.

Stunts

a. half line slant

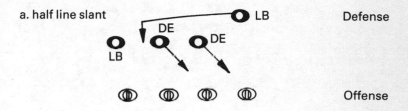

b. loop manoeuvre

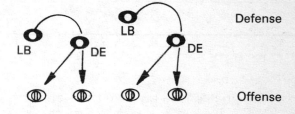

Underneath coverage
The area in the Defense between the Linebackers and the Defensive secondary.

Undershift
The opposite to overshift, this is a Defensive formation of placing less men to that side, in anticipation of an Offensive play.

Zone coverage

A Defensive formation in which the defending players will allow a Receiver to enter and exit his zone without following.

Zone Coverage

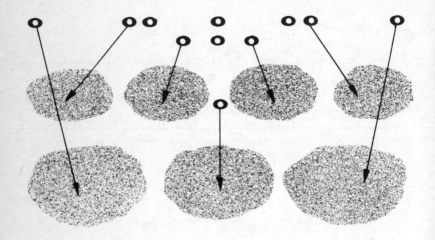

Zone

A designated area given to the Defensive secondary and Linebackers to cover against the pass.

Special Teams

Holder
A Special Teams' player who receives the snap from
the Center, and positions the ball for the Kicker on
Field Goal and PAT attempts.

On-side kick
A short kickoff, designed to give the kicking team a
good chance of immediate recovery, it has to travel a
minimum of ten yards down field.

Overloading
The movement of extra players to one side of the
Kicking team's front line.

Place Kicker
A Special Teams' player whose specific responsibility is
for kickoffs, Field Goals and extra point attempts.

Punter
A Special Teams' player whose specific responsibility is
to kick the ball from hands, as far down the field and
so gaining as much yardage as possible, this play is
usually made on a fourth down situation.

Return men
Players in the special team, assigned to run back
kickoffs and punts.

Wedge
A formation used on kickoff returns, by potential
Blockers and protectors of the ball carrier.

Field, Timing and Officials

The Field of Play

The American Football field is 120 yards long by 53⅓ yards wide. The actual playing area is 100 yards long with 2 additional 10 yard end zones, at either end of the field. The sidelines limit the field's width and the endlines limit its length. The endlines are where the goalposts are positioned centrally. The function of the goalposts is for Field Goals and Points After Touchdown attempts. Parallel to the goal lines are the yard lines, which are marked every 5 yards and are numbered every 10 yards up to the half way line, ie the 50 yard line, in other words the numbering goes 10, 20, 30, 40, 50, 40, 30, 20, 10.

Alongside these numbers is an arrow pointing in the direction closest to the endline. Running up the centre of the field is a set of parallel dotted lines called hashmarks located 70' 9" from each sideline and 18 feet apart. The hashmarks run from goal line to goal line and define the area from within which the ball has to be played from any down. The hashmarks are 1 yard apart. By marking the field in this manner players and spectators alike can easily see where their team is positioned at any time during a drive. The general appearance of the field gives the game its popular name of gridiron.

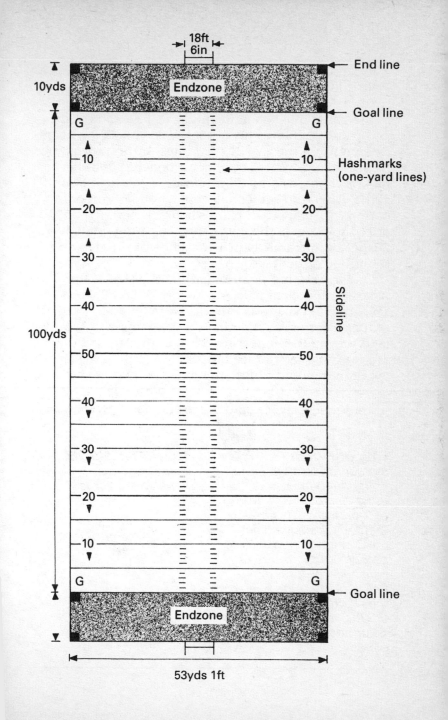

In addition to the markings on the field of play is a yellow line set 6' outside the field completely surrounding its border. Everyone who is not playing in the game must stand behind this line and coaches and players situated on the sidelines must stay in an area between the two 32 yard lines, during the game. In this area is located the teams' benches and these must not be positioned any closer to the field than 10 yards. This is to protect players who may run out of bounds. Usually each team's bench is situated on opposite sides of the field, however if the home team wishes both teams' benches may be positioned on the same side of the field.

One interesting point regarding the size of the American Football field is its width of 53 1/3 yards. This unusual size was introduced in an attempt to reduce injuries, by opening up the game with a larger field during its pioneering times in the late 1880's. Walter Camp introduced this size, as it was the largest space that would fit into the new stadium at Harvard.

LAW-BREAKER
In addition to all the time limits the offensive team must also deal with the 30 second clock. This means that the Offensive team must begin play within 30 seconds of the referee's whistle indicating that the ball is ready to be played. If the Offensive team fails to do this, they will be penalised by a 5 yard penalty.

THE REFEREE'S DECISION
Delay of game
Penalty — 5 yards

Timing

The American Football game lasts 60 minutes and is split into 4 x 15 minute quarters. Separating the second and third quarters, ie half-time, is a 15 minute break and there is also a 2 minute break, separating the first and second quarters and the third and fourth quarters. This 2 minute break is to allow the teams to change ends. By changing ends in this manner, ie. at the end of every quarter neither team can gain any advantage from weather conditions such as wind or sun. In addition to the breaks mentioned, each team is allowed

LAW-BREAKER
When a team requests a time out after having already taken their three time outs allowed for that half. a) when the Offensive team takes more than 30 seconds to put the ball in play after it has been declared ready for play by the referee. b) when a player crawls or attempts to deliberately advance the ball after it has been called dead. c) when a team deliberately attempts to conserve or consume time by using tactics obviously unfair. In this instance the referee shall order the game clock to be started or stopped, depending upon the situation.

THE REFEREE'S DECISION
Delay of game
Penalty — 5 yards

LAW-BREAKER

After a dead ball has been declared ready for play by the referee it becomes a live ball when it has been legally snapped. The ball shall be put into play within 30 seconds after it has been declared ready for play by the referee, however if play has been suspended during this time, for example an unfair crowd noise situation the 30 second count will be recommenced.

THE REFEREE'S DECISION
Delay of game
Penalty — 5 yards

3 x 90 second time outs during each half. During each time out the game clock is stopped. Time outs are usually called on the field by a team's Offensive or Defensive captain but the officials can also call time out to assess penalties, measure yardage, tend to injured players, replace equipment and to inform the coaches that 2 minutes remain at the end of the second and fourth quarter. This information is called the 2 minute warning.

LAW-BREAKER

Each team must ensure that its players are on the field of play at the scheduled time for the beginning of each half.

THE REFEREE'S DECISION
Delay of game
Penalty — 5 yards

The playing roster

On game day, each team is allowed a maximum of 45 players eligible to play. From this 45 players, units of 11 men are organised into Defense, Offense and Special Teams. Only 11 of the 45 players available can be on the field at any one time. Until as recently as 1972 players in the NFL could wear any number, but now their numbers relate to the positions in which they play.

   1-19 Quarterbacks and Kickers.
   20-49 Running Backs and Defensive Backs.
   50-59 Centers and Linebackers.
   60-79 Defensive Linemen and Interior Offensive
         Linemen.
   80-89 Wide Receivers and Tight Ends.
   90-99 Defensive Linemen.

LAW-BREAKER
Whilst the ball is in play, coaches, substitute players and authorised attendants of the team may not stray from their designated team area. The head coach will be given 2 official warnings before a penalty is imposed, initially a 5 yard penalty, the penalty will be increased to 15 yards if the violation continues.

THE REFEREE'S DECISION
Sideline interference
Unsportmanlike conduct
Penalty — 5-15 yards

Because of the limit imposed regarding the number of players available on each game day, teams have to impose their own limitations on players to position.

A typical 45 man NFL roster would break down something like this

Offensive Linemen – 8	Linebackers – 8
Defensive Linemen – 6	Defensive Backs – 7
Quarterbacks – 3	Kicker – 1
Receivers – 6	Punter – 1
Running Backs – 5	Total – 45.

LAW-BREAKER
Any number of legal substitutes for either team may enter the game between quarters, after a score or during the interval between downs, only for the purpose of replacing a player or players. a) no substitution can be made whilst the ball is in play. b) an incoming substitute must enter the field from his team's area sideline. Likewise a substituted player must depart from the field to his team's area on the side line. c) incoming substitutes must remain in the game for at least one play and replaced players must stay out of the game for at least one play.

THE REFEREE'S DECISION
*Substitution infraction
Penalty – 15 yards
and down repeated*

LAW-BREAKER
*The referee
shall hold a coaches'
conference when tactics are
considered to be unfair.*

**THE REFEREE'S
DECISION**
*Delay of game
Penalty — 5 yards*

The officials

Unlike the British game of Soccer, in which there is
one referee and two linesmen to control the game,
American Football has 7 officials on the field of play.

The officials are jointly responsible for the
enforcement of all rules and must co-operate closely in
ensuring that the rules are adhered to. Each official has
a different responsibility outlined briefly below.

The referee

He has general control of the game. He is the sole
authority for the score and his decisions are final upon
all rules.

The umpire

He has primary jurisdiction over the equipment and
conduct of the players.

The linesman

His primary jurisdiction is over the neutral zone and
infractions of the scrimmage formation.

The field judge, back judge, side judge and line judge

They are responsible for covering plays down field and
towards the sidelines. One of these judges will have
primary jurisdiction over the timing of the game. He
will also act for the referee on down field play.

LAW-BREAKER

No player, substitute, coach or authorised attendant within the team area shall act in an unsportsmanlike manner that may interfere with the orderly game administration, either during the game or between periods, eg. i) no player, substitute, coach or authorised attendant shall use abusive or insulting language to opposing players, substitutes, coaches or officials. ii) no team attendant may come on to the field of play to attend to an injured player unless acknowledged by an official. iii) at the end of a play or a score the player must either leave the ball near the dead ball spot or return it to the official. This prohibits taking the ball off the field of play, kicking or throwing the ball any distance that requires the official to retrieve it, throwing the ball high into the air and into the stands, or acting in any other unsportsmanlike manner that may delay the game.

iv) no player, substitute, coach or authorised attendant shall use language or gestures that may provoke ill-will. v) no player substitute may enter the field for any purpose other than to replace a player. vi) no player already disqualified from the game should re-enter the field of play.

THE REFEREE'S DECISION

Unsportsmanlike conduct Penalty — 15 yards

EQUIPMENT

American Football is a tough game, and in 1905 eighteen players died, as a result of injuries on the field. Since then it has been compulsory for players in the United States and Canada to wear 'protective body armour' known as pads, when they play.

The diagram shows where and what the players use, but a brief description might help to understand how it all fits together.

The girdle shell is like a pair of tight fitting shorts and contains and supports the hip pads which protect against heavy tackles from the side, and the spine protector which supports and protects the coccyx. The thigh and knee pads are slotted into pockets in the playing trousers. Most people are aware of how vulnerable knee joints can be, but until you have been pummelled in the thigh by the head of a fifteen stone opponent with his full body weight behind the charge, you might think that

LAW-BREAKER
Players are prohibited from being equipped with any electronic device for the purpose of communicating with the coach or coaching staff.

THE REFEREE'S DECISION
Failure to wear required equipment.
Time-out charged to offending team

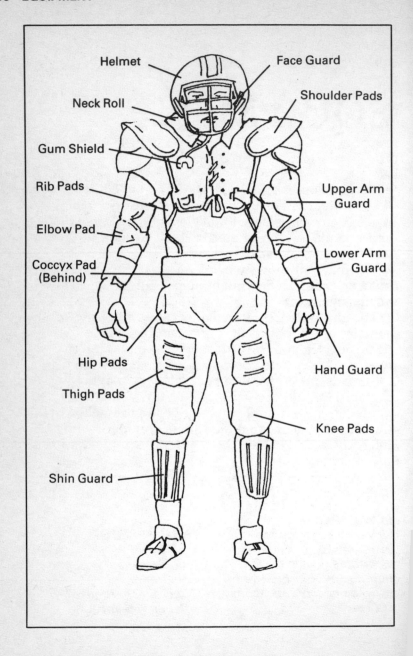

Helmet

Face Guard

Neck Roll

Shoulder Pads

Gum Shield

Rib Pads

Upper Arm
Guard

Elbow Pad

Coccyx Pad
(Behind)

Lower Arm
Guard

Hip Pads

Thigh Pads

Hand Guard

Knee Pads

Shin Guard

the thigh protector is unnecessary. The most obvious and most often talked about pieces of protective equipment are the shoulder pads. These are also the most important. They offer three way protection. Firstly a foam neck collar protects the neck from injury by restricting backwards and sideways head movement. The cantilevered epaulets lying over the shoulders, protect both them and the collar bone. The ribs are protected by chest plates pulled over the head, front and back.

The shirt bears the number each player must display

LAW-BREAKER

No player shall conceal the ball beneath his clothing or substitute any other article in place of the ball.

THE REFEREE'S DECISION
Unsportsmanlike conduct Penalty — 15 yards

LAW-BREAKER
No player should wear equipment that is considered to be dangerous or hazardous to an opponent.
Eg. projection of metal or other hard substance from a player's person or clothing. Football boot studs (known as cleats), may not be more than ½" in length nor made of a material which is liable to chip or fracture, or made from a metal substance.

THE REFEREE'S DECISION
Failure to wear required equipment.
Time-out charged to offending team

so that he can be identified by the officials and keeps the free moving parts of the shoulder pads from impeding the player's movement. In addition Linemen usually wear forearm and hand pads to protect muscles and bones. These pads are designed not to interfere with the articulation of the wrist, while still supporting it.

Finally, everyone knows the helmet is essential. It is heavily padded inside the shell to lessen the risk of concussion and internal bleeding from impact injuries. The shell itself hopefully protects the skull from fracture. Attached to the helmet, a steel faceguard protects the eyes, nose, mouth and jawbone. Players will also wear a gumshield.

LAW-BREAKER
All players shall wear mandatory equipment which must have been professionally manufactured and not altered to decrease protection.

THE REFEREE'S DECISION
Failure to wear required equipment.
Time-out charged to offending team

FITNESS

There is a popular misconception that you need to be over 6 feet tall and weigh 15 stone to play American Football. In fact, people of all shapes and sizes can play the game successfully and contribute to the team, provided that they are not overweight for their build, and are fit.

There is no doubt that American Football makes terrific demands on the body and you will need strength, stamina, flexibility and speed for every position on the field.

Most organized teams will arrange their own fitness and training programmes with carefully constructed exercises tailored for individual positions. Usually, they will also offer supervised endurance training and possibly weight training, under strict guidance from a properly qualified instructor.

Young people are naturally fit, and should not consider weight or endurance training until their bones have stopped growing. Unsupervised training of this kind can cause all kinds of injuries which can take a long time to heal and cause serious problems later.

However, as with any sport it is very important to warm up properly before you start any exertions. Cold muscles are very easily damaged. It is also very important to stretch the muscles and improve your flexibility.

We offer a selection of simple exercises to stretch specific areas of the body. If you practise them regularly you will notice an enormous improvement in your game and will be helping yourself to avoid injury.

In addition we include a few exercises for building resistance to injury and improving stamina in those areas most vulnerable in the game.

As with all exercise, do not overdo it to begin with. Warm up with a little gentle jogging before you start, and cool down slowly afterwards. Put on a tracksuit or other warm clothing to avoid chills and cooling muscles too quickly. If at any time you feel sick or dizzy stop at once.

Flexibility

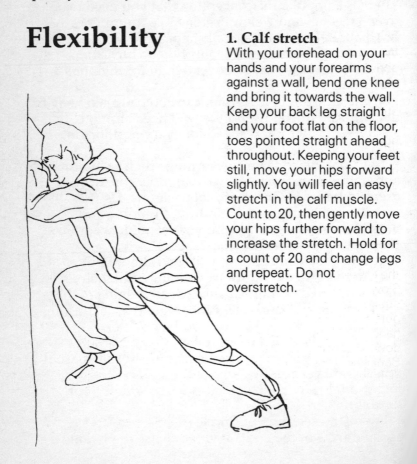

1. Calf stretch

With your forehead on your hands and your forearms against a wall, bend one knee and bring it towards the wall. Keep your back leg straight and your foot flat on the floor, toes pointed straight ahead throughout. Keeping your feet still, move your hips forward slightly. You will feel an easy stretch in the calf muscle. Count to 20, then gently move your hips further forward to increase the stretch. Hold for a count of 20 and change legs and repeat. Do not overstretch.

2. Groin stretch

With feet wide apart and upper body straight, take your weight on one leg and bend the other, in a lunge. Hold for a count of 15 then transfer your weight to the other leg and repeat.

3. Jack-knife stretch

With feet together and back and legs straight, bend slowly from your hips, until you feel a slight stretch in the ham string. Hold for a count of ten. Do not force this, it should not hurt either your ham string or your lower back. Bring your head up slowly first, to avoid dizziness.

4. Hurdler's stretch

Bring one leg forward, with your heel on the floor. Bend the other leg behind you. Slowly, keeping your body straight try to touch your outstretched foot with your hand and bend your head down towards your knee. Count to 15 while you feel a slight pull behind your knee.

Then lean back, until your shoulders are on the floor. Try to keep your leg straight and the bent knee flat on the floor. Count to 15. Change legs and repeat.

5. Back stretch

Lie down flat on the floor and bring your straight legs, feet together, up until your body weight is mainly over your shoulders. Support your hips with your hands and hold for a count of 15. Gradually bring your legs, still straight, over your head to touch the floor and hold for a further count of 15. Bring your legs back slowly, rolling down flat, shoulders and back first until your feet touch the ground. Do not swing back to the starting position.

6. Neck stretch

With both knees bent and feet flat on the floor, interlace your fingers behind your head at ear level. Use your arms to pull your head slowly forwards until you feel a slight stretch in your neck. Count to 5 and return slowly to the starting position. Repeat 4 times.

7. Shoulder blade pinch

Pull your shoulder blades back together to create tension in your upper back. Hold for a count of 5 and relax. Gently pull your head forward as in number 6. Repeat 3 times.

8. Shoulder stretch

Extend arms overhead with palms together. Stretch arms upwards and slightly backwards. Breathe in as you pull up, hold for a count of 7, breathe out and relax.

10. Shoulder stretch 3

With your arms overhead, hold one elbow with the opposite hand. Gently pull the elbow behind your head slowly, hold the stretch for 15 seconds.

9. Shoulder stretch 2

Gently pull your elbow across your chest towards your opposite shoulder. Hold for a count of 10.

11. Star jumps

Try to do about 20 star jumps for improved leg and arm flexibility.

Stamina

1. Push ups
Lie down on your front with arms bent and hands at your shoulders. Push up straightening your arms, taking your body weight on your arms and toes. Lower your chest to the floor, then push up again.

2. High stepping
To increase speed and stamina lay out six tyres or other obstacles which you can step in and out of.

Adopting the sprinters stance run as fast as you can putting your feet alternately into the tyres bringing your knees up as high as possible.

3. North/South/East/West

For 2 players

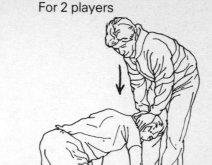

One player stands and the other kneels on all fours facing the standing player's knees.

The kneeler pushes his head up using his neck muscles, whilst the standing player gently offers resistance to the push with his palms flat on the top of the kneeler's head.

The Stander then cups his hands under the chin of the kneeler who tries to push his head down. The stander offers resistance to the push.

Then the kneeler pushes his head against the outside of the leg of the stander. The stander stands firm offering resistance to the push.

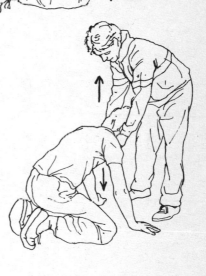

The kneeler then pushes against the outside of the other leg in the same way.

Then the players change places and repeat the exercise.